Emma and Enchanted Easter Basket

THE MAGIC OF EASTER COMES FROM THE JOY WE SHARE!

DEDICATED TO JP, THE ONE WHO MAKES MY DREAMS COME TRUE AND SHOWS ME THE WAY

WRITTEN BY

NICOLE BLAKE-MERSINIA

Emma wakes up early on Easter morning. The sun peeks through her window, and she bounces out of bed. Today is the day! Easter!

She dresses up and rushes downstairs and gasps. Right there on the table sits a beautiful Easter basket, wrapped in decorative pink linen and filled with colorful eggs, chocolates, and a soft, fluffy bunny.

"Wow!" Emma says, grabbing a handful of jellybeans. But as she digs deeper into the basket, she finds something unusual at the bottom.

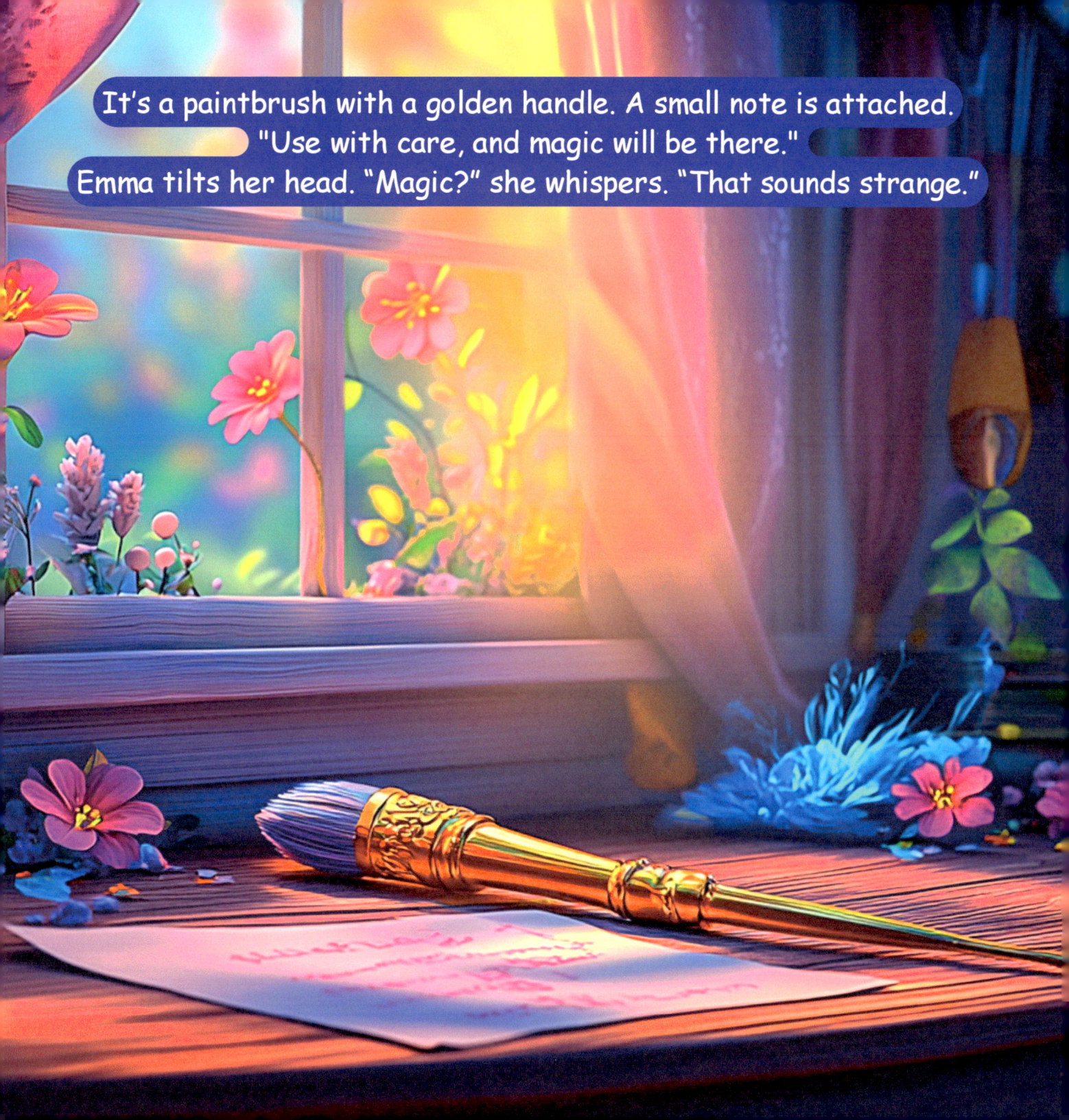

But she's curious. She grabs one of the plain white eggs from her basket and dips the brush into her watercolor set. Carefully, she paints a blue butterfly on the egg.

As soon as she finishes the last wing, the egg wiggles in her hand.
"Uh-oh…" Emma says.
POOF!
The butterfly flutters off the egg, flapping its wings in the air!

Emma's mouth drops open. "No way!" She reaches out, but the butterfly zooms past her nose, twirling in circles. She giggles. "Okay, that was cool! Let's try something else."

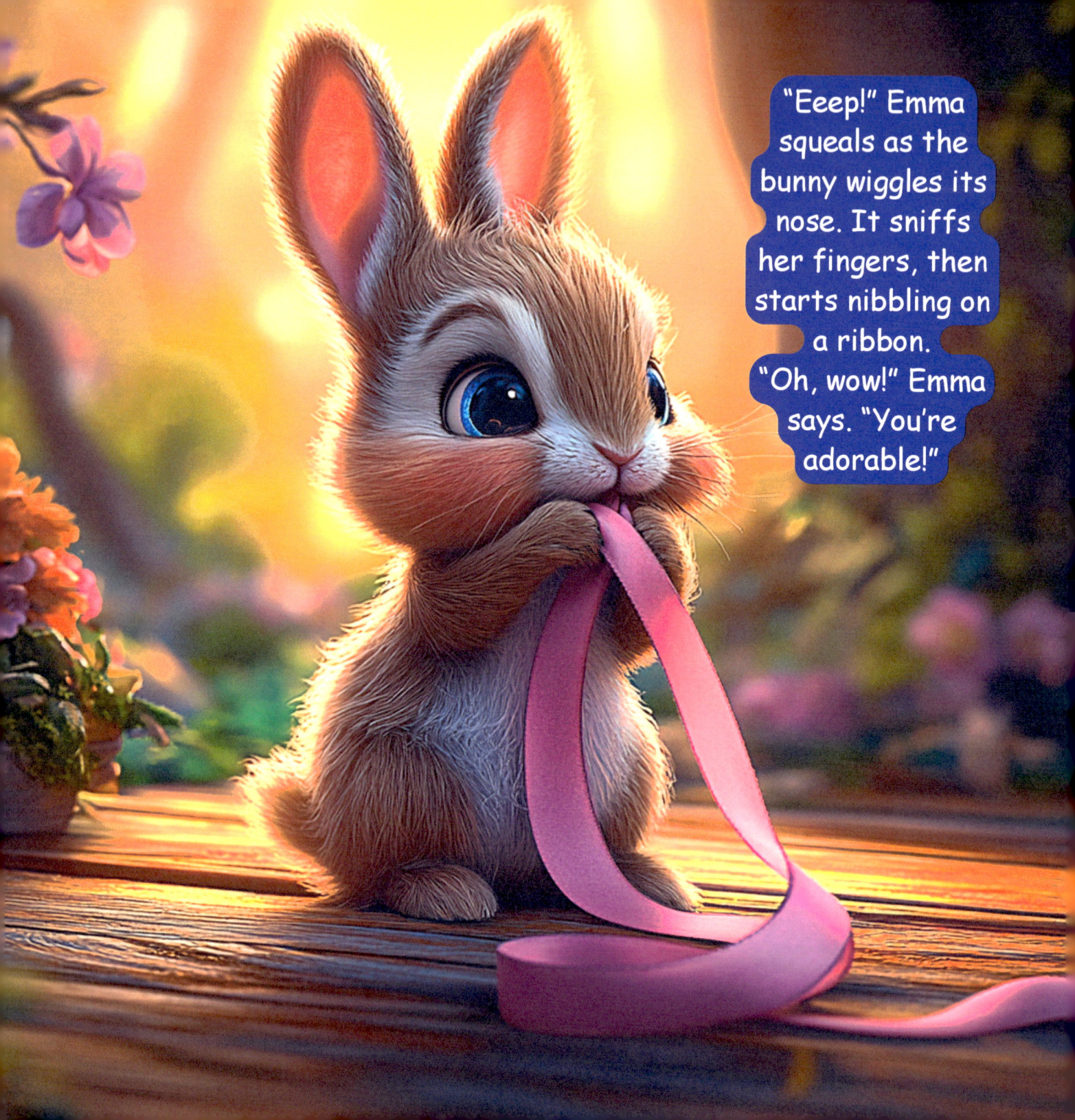

But she's not done experimenting yet. She grabs her plate and quickly paints a few jellybeans on it. BOING! BOING! BOING! The jellybeans pop to life and start bouncing everywhere!

"Oh no!" Emma says, ducking as jellybeans bounce around the kitchen. "This is getting crazy!"
She tries to catch them, but they bounce too fast.

"I need to fix this," Emma says. Then she has an idea. "I'll paint something bigger!" She grabs a marshmallow chick from her basket and paints an even bigger chick on a napkin. POOF! A giant pink marshmallow chick appears!

It waddles forward, its squishy feet making little plop, plop sounds on the floor.

"Oh no... you're HUGE!" Emma says, stepping back.

The marshmallow chick bumps into a chair, then flops onto its belly like a pillow.

The bunny hops onto its back. The butterfly lands on its soft head. The jellybeans keep bouncing like tiny jumping beans. This is a disaster!

She quickly paints a basket—and whoosh! The bouncing jellybeans hop inside and turn back into regular candy.

The only thing left is the butterfly, fluttering near the window. Emma smiles and whispers, "You can stay."
She gently opens the window, and the butterfly flies off into the blue sky.

As she picks up her Easter basket, she notices one last golden egg inside. She cracks it open and finds a note.

"Magic is fun, but life is already full of wonders. You don't need magic to have an amazing day!"

Emma grins and looks around.
Her Easter basket is still full of chocolates and treats. The sun is shining through the window. Birds are chirping outside.

She didn't need bouncing jellybeans or giant marshmallow chicks to make today special. It already was.

Emma pops a jellybean in her mouth, leans back in her chair, and smiles. "This was the best Easter ever," she says. "Even without the magic."

The End.

Now for some coloring pages

What's Next
Scan the QR code to check out the other books in this Series

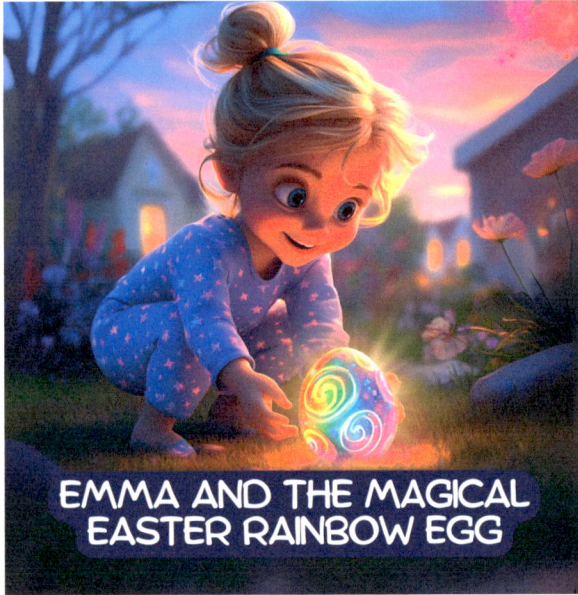

EMMA AND THE MAGICAL EASTER RAINBOW EGG

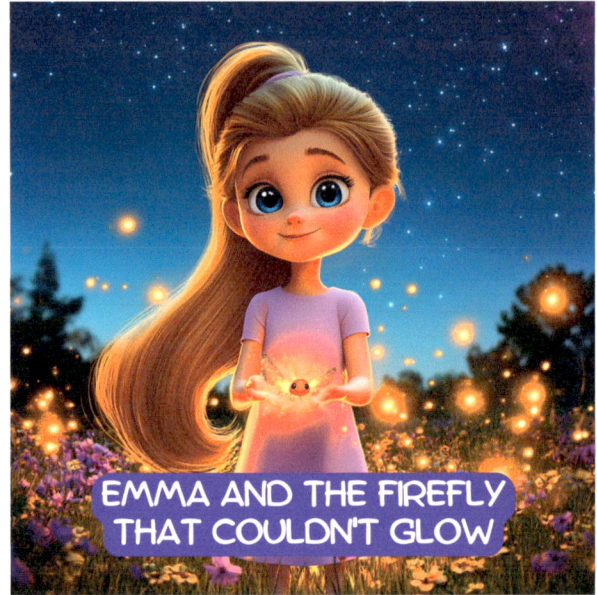

EMMA AND THE FIREFLY THAT COULDN'T GLOW

Scan me

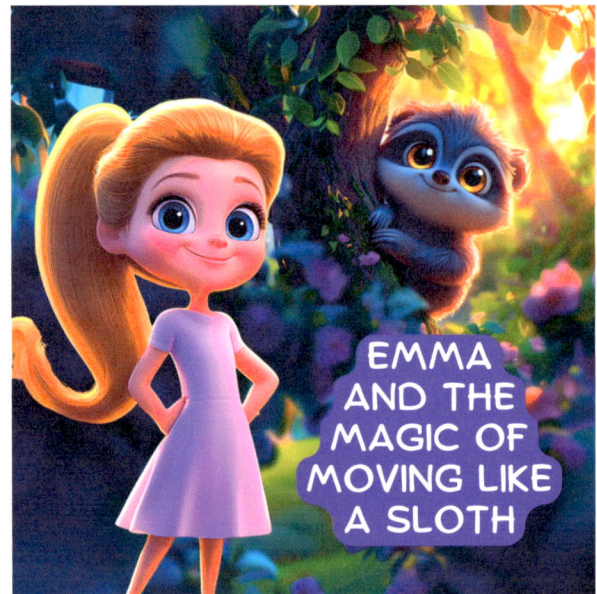

EMMA AND THE MAGIC OF MOVING LIKE A SLOTH

What's Next
Scan the QR code to check out the other books in this Series

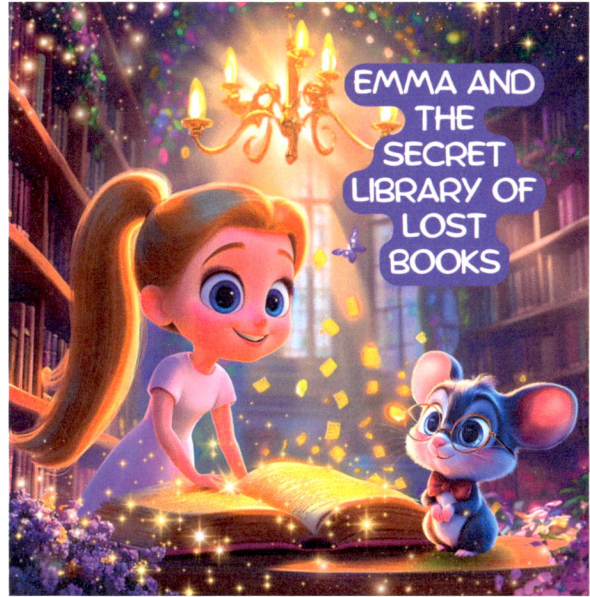

Scan me

About the Author

Nicole Blake-Mersinia is a passionate children's book author who weaves heartwarming tales that spark imagination and inspire young minds. With a talent for storytelling and a deep understanding of childhood wonder, Nicole creates vibrant worlds filled with adventure, friendship, and valuable life lessons.

Her stories are known for their relatable characters and enchanting narratives that resonate with both children and parents alike.

When she's not writing, Nicole enjoys exploring nature, drawing inspiration from the world around her. She believes in the magic of storytelling and its power to shape young minds.

Through her books, Nicole hopes to inspire curiosity, courage, and kindness in every young reader, encouraging them to dream big and believe in the impossible.